Baby journal and record book

This book is all about

a letter to my baby

waiting for you

your due date

your birth day

How we found out we were expecting you

How we felt about your arrival

When we heard your first heartbeat

When we felt you move for the first time

When we saw you on the ultrasound scan

favorite girls' names

reasons we like them

favorite boys' names

reasons we like them

colors for your nursery

themes/decor for your nursery

details of your nursery

where and when

guest list

gifts

your birth

your birth

date   time

where

weight   length

who was present

hair color   eye color

who did you look like

your birth story

first visitors

birth announcement

your footprint

your handprint

taking you home from the hospital

your first day and night at home

your first bath

you first focused

you first lifted your head

you first held an object

you first found your hands

you first found your feet

you first smiled

you first laughed

your first word

you first rolled over

you first sat up

you first crawled

you first pointed

you first clapped

you first waved

you first stood up

you first walked

you tried your first solids

what you tried

your reaction

you first fed yourself

you first used a highchair

you first used a cup

food you loved and food you disliked

you first

you first used a highchair

you first used a cup

food you loved

food you disliked

playtime

your favorite toys

your favorite soft toys

your favorite books

your favorite nursery rhymes and lullabies

your favorite songs

your favorite shows

your favorite games

your favorite baby groups

celebrations

celebrations in your first year

your first birthday

where and when

guest list

decorations and theme

entertainment and games

food and drinks

gifts

your first christmas

where and who with

gifts you received

your first vacation

where and when

what we did

favorite memories

favorite memories of your first year

www.ingramcontent.com/pod-product-compliance
Lightning Source LLC
Chambersburg PA
CBHW042002070526

44584CB00005BA/316